TOR

I0019474

Access the Dark Net

Stay Anonymous Online and Escape NSA Spying

Evan Lane

Contents

Chapter 1

What is Tor?

Tor is an internet browser comprised of several networks of servers that can conceal online activities from anyone who may be watching. Tor (The Onion Router), is operated solely by volunteers dedicated to protecting the privacy of internet users all over the world. Tor uses a series of virtual tunnels making it nearly impossible for anyone to see what websites or products one may be searching online. There is no direct connection to any IP address or webpage keeping your virtual identity a complete secret. Any information one might share online via social media, blogs or anything of the like will not need to worry about invasion of privacy. Users of Tor will have access to websites they may not otherwise have access to. This is especially useful for those traveling abroad or living in countries that limit access to certain websites.

Tor helps to protect against online surveillance, which is also referred to as traffic analysis. Traffic analysis works by keeping track of the websites you visit and then advertises to you specifically. Have you ever noticed that ads to a website you visited previously will appear on the right-hand side of your email inbox or other websites you might be visiting? That is because of traffic analysis. Companies pay for traffic analysis so they can figure out who to target in the way of advertisement. Anything searched over a public network is subject to traffic analysis. The use of Tor eliminates this kind of analysis and allows users to roam freely without those pesky advertisements popping up at every turn.

There are several different destinations and sources of traffic occurring on the internet that allows others to track interests and behaviors. Not only does this make it easy for marketing companies to send ads to you based on your searches, but it also makes it easier for hackers to access your searches. This is a criminal activity in which they look into your social media accounts to see if you are on vacation so they can rob the home. Hackers can also literally wreak havoc by destroying credit scores and discovering an exact location. While the Dark Net sounds daunting, it is really a great place for people to browse the internet and post freely without having to fear being monitored.

Use of a public internet like Internet Explorer, Firefox or Google Chrome makes it easy for data to be collected in what are known as packets. Internet analysis occurs when the packets are broken down. From there comes the payload, which is the data that was collected as well as the header that directs traffic online. Payload information is what is embedded in emails, audio files or standard webpages. The payload is usually encrypted, but the traffic analysis tends to expose the majority of the information of what is being explored on the internet. The header is what traffic analysis focuses on because it will show the source, time, ultimate destination (webpage you ended up on) and the size of files discovered on the internet.

Downloading Tor is a very simple process. There is no program to purchase nor is there any lengthy instructions to follow. If one wishes to use the Dark Net, all they need to do is download the Tor browser. This can be done easily by visiting www.torproject.org/download.download. Once you've arrived at the webpage, it will provide all sorts of useful information on how to properly use the Dark Net and any system requirements necessary for proper use of the browser. Once the Tor browser has been downloaded, simply do what you have always done on the internet except now you can do so worry free!

Tor can be used the minute the download is complete. Tor is one of the most secure browsers in the world, and it is good to know that there are government agencies all over the world who keep an eye on Tor. The Federal Bureau of Investigation is included. As a matter of fact, the FBI admittedly attempted a malware attack on Tor, which was unsuccessful.

Naturally, as with anything, there are also weaknesses with the Tor browser. However, to this day, it has not been penetrated or taken down by any malicious attack. When used properly, any activity online will be hidden by the hidden networks utilized with the Tor browser.

Computers using Tor are less likely to be attacked or compromised. There are other steps one can take to keep your online activities completely hidden.

First, Tor recommends *not* using Windows, which includes the use of Tor bundles. Specifically, the Tor bundles have weaknesses that were targeted by the FBI a few years ago, in their attempted attack on the Tor networks. Workstations should not be created while using Linux in conjunction with Tor. There needs to be a proxy (the best is Privoxy) used in addition to browsers with a firewall for any data that might be visible outside of the browser's protection. One can use Clearnet, but if that fails, Whonix or Tails are great to keep all data from being leaked. You will always want to have a firewall to ensure third parties are unable to access data to perform the traffic analysis we discussed previously.

If you are using external (or even internal) storage, you will want to ensure encryption. Currently, the LUKS program is great for this and is one of the options that will pop up while you are installing the Tor browser.

When using Tor, always make sure that your computer is up to date. Any time you are prompted to run updates, do so to keep Tor working properly and to make sure your version of Tor is always up to date. This allows the user to avoid new security breaches as well as using their workstations. If it seems like it has been a while since the last update, you can always double check the Tor site to see if there have been any new software updates that need to be downloaded. You will not want to miss any of those so the computer and internet browsers will always be properly protected.

While a lot of programs you might use require Java or Flash, you are going to want to disable those. While using Tor, you might come across a website that says those programs are required. The use of either of those allows for traffic analysis. Most of the things you see with Java or Flash are not anything important. It tends to be a Gif or something along those lines that can easily be ignored and are not required for you to access a website fully. If, for some reason, you absolutely do need to enable scripting, do so temporarily and make sure you disable it again before leaving the site.

Rid your computer of cookies or data that a website may send to the advertisers. This is a manual step required as there is no way for the Dark Net to complete it for you. You will see an add-on called *self-destructing cookies* that will automatically destroy all cookies on your computer.

It is also a good idea to use a laptop as your main workstation because it is mobile. Additionally, laptops are a little easier to discard in the instance that becomes a necessity. Finally, avoid using Google when possible. It is one of the most commonly used search engines all over the world meaning it is the most heavily watched in the way of traffic analysis.

While using Tor, the environment used along with it is also important. A little later, we are going to talk about some of the weaknesses of Tor, which is why the environment is important. There are some things you can do to make sure that hackers or traffic analysis don't occur.

1. As mentioned, a laptop is the best type of computer to use because it is mobile. It is best to use Tor anywhere except home. Specifically, this is when you are searching information that could be considered

sensitive. Public networks are easier to monitor, but by using Tor and the fact that there are several thousand people using public networks in your area, you will be much safer online. Hackers are usually able to connect to your computer without your knowing, which is another reason the Tor network is so great. If you do not use Tor at home, you will not be tied to a location, making it more difficult for hackers to find any personal information about you. If advanced threats are a fear of yours, take your laptop to a coffee shop for any internet browsing you may wish to do. However, Tor networks are near impenetrable so using them at home is safe so long as you are not worried about what kind of information you are searching online or what kind of things you are posting on any social media accounts you may have.

2. Online activities in which you do not wish to be tracked and you have chosen to leave the

house, remember to leave your cell phone at home. If, for some reason, you believe your online activities are being tracked, your cell phone (turned on) at home will lead others to believe you are at home and they will attempt to look into the IP address associated with your house. If you leave your phone at home, it is a good idea to make sure people know what time you are expected to return so there are no concerns if they attempt to call several times and are unable to reach you. Likewise, there are messaging applications you can use over Tor that are not traceable and you should be able to communicate with people through those messaging apps.

3. It is always wise to monitor how much time you are spending in one location while using Tor. There are some hackers (or government agencies) who look for people that are using public networks. It is recommended to avoid using the same

public location on a regular basis. Try to set up several places like Starbucks, McDonalds and any other place that offers free Wi-Fi so there is no way to tie you to any one location. The best protocol is to use a location once and then never go back. That is incredibly difficult for people who have no car or live in a small town with fewer choices as far as free Wi-Fi is concerned. Continuing to use the same location makes it easier for the people who work there and those who frequent the location to remember what you look like, the kind of car you drive and so on. Always keep in mind that people who work in those places tend to start to recognize regulars and it is best if you can mix up locations and not go back at all, or at the very most every few weeks.

With those recommendations, out of the way, we are going to talk a little about the fear of using the Dark Net. The name itself sounds daunting, almost illegal, right? There is not anything to worry about. It is actually very safe and legal. Making sure you have a positive outlook when it comes to Tor is going to be crucial. It will also make you feel more at ease while using Tor. Below are some more steps on how to use Tor and feel safe while doing so.

1. It is a good idea to create an online persona or virtual identity while using Tor. Use something that will not be tied to you in any way. For instance, do not use any moniker you have used anywhere in the past and avoid using any variation of your name or personal email address. Likewise, you are going to want to create a new email address that you use specifically for Tor. Again, make sure you do not use your name or any part of it while creating an email address you use on Tor. Ultimately, you are separating your personal life from your Tor life. It is kind of cool when you think about it that way.

2. Make all new accounts with your new virtual identity and be very careful not to get your virtual accounts and personal accounts mixed up.

3. Try not to use your virtual accounts on Clearnet unless there is no other option.

4. Earlier we talked about leaving your personal cell phone at home if you are going to use a public network to access Tor. Along those lines, it is wise to have a disposable phone for any phone calls or text messages you may want to send while using the Tor network. Believe it or not, your cell phone can be tracked easily. If you choose to use a disposable phone, make sure your personal phone is turned off while using Tor for an added safeguard. When purchasing a disposable phone, use cash and not a debit or credit card. Also, remember to never use a SIM card on the phone nor should you activate it near your home address. This

should be used in conjunction with your virtual identity and kept separate from anything to do with your personal life. That point cannot be driven home enough. The phone and Dark Net identity should absolutely be kept separate.

Tor is great for keeping online activities secret because of the increased privacy and security associated with using the Dark Net. This is great for keeping hackers or government agencies from looking into your online activities. Sometimes, you're using a virtual identity may raise some red flags, which is another reason you want to keep personal life matters separate. This includes family members.

Chapter 2

Browsing the Internet Anonymously with a VPN

Internet privacy is a concern for everyone this day and age. Most people would like to know just how secure their activities online are and how much of the things they browse are traced back to their IP address. To be perfectly honest, as we previously touched on, everything done online can be traced back to the user. Whether one uses public or private Wi-Fi, anything that is searched online can be traced to the device you use and therefore linked to you directly. While most people are not engaging in any illegal activities, it is quite disturbing to know that anyone can look at what we are doing online at any given moment. There are millions and millions of other people using the internet who choose not to take special precautions. Without taking the extra step to protect your online activities, anyone from the

NSA, FBI, and general hackers can see what you search while on the internet.

One of the questions you might be asking right about now is, how can internet activity be traced to you personally? The answer to that is quite simple. It is the IP address that is tied to your device. The IP is a code uniquely associated with your devices that are network enabled. It gives internet servers a general location of where you are geographically. Each time you are accessing an online service or website, the IP address must pass through those servers, making your activity visible to those hackers and marketers we discussed earlier.

Any information that passes through these servers simply lets them know which language should be displayed on the website, what content the user is going to have access to and whatever advertisements they deem relevant to your specific search. Overseas, content can be limited and therefore limit your access to information based on the location the IP provides. Also, there are websites that draw attention from law enforcement agencies worldwide. Specifically, websites such as those related to pornography or BitTorrent.

There are some ways to hide your online activities and, in this chapter, we are going to specifically address the use of a VPN along with Tor.

A VPN is an abbreviation for Virtual Private Network. This allows a connection to any internet service through your personal server by a provider of the VPN. Information going from your tablet, phone, or computer through the BPN server is encrypted. By using the BPN. You are provided additional privacy by hiding your internet activities from the Internet Service Provider (ISP) and anyone else who may be looking in on your activity. Using a VPN in addition to the Tor network allows users to avoid censorship while at work, school, the government, and even the internet service provider. The use of a VPN creates what is known as a *geospoof* of your actual location meaning you can have access to many services that might have previously been denied. This usually happens if you are traveling outside of the United States or perhaps if you are in a geographical location that prohibits access to certain websites. The added security of a VPN can also keep you protected against hackers if you are using a public Wi-Fi network. It also lets the user download anything safely.

Anyone can get a subscription to a VPN and we are going to go over exactly how they work. The user will sign up for a service plan with a company of their choice. There are quite a few VPN services and later in this chapter, we will talk about some choices you have in regards to selecting the one that will be right for you. Once the user is on a service plan, they will be able to download software and any applications necessary to run the software on their device or devices. From there, the user can select a location for their server and quite easily connect. The VPN hides the IP address and you will be assigned on specifically associated with the server chosen when you signed up for the service. Internet activity is encrypted and entirely hidden from everyone so you are free to use the network you have set up as well as any public networks without having to worry that the pages you are searching can be traced back to you.

When you are considering selecting a VPN, it is important to search for specific features surrounding connectivity and security. The first step is finding a VPN that has the bandwidth you desire. Bandwidth functions by data transfer limits, which are usually imposed by the ISP in addition to the VPN you have selected. Most VPNs have unlimited bandwidth. While looking for the VPN that is right for you, just double check to make sure there are no bandwidth limits as those tend to slow down internet browsing.

Next, select a VPN with several different connections. Because most people use many different devices from smartphones to laptops and tablets, you are going to want to choose a VPN that allows you to connect all your devices.

Lastly, you are going to check the strength of the encryption of the VPN. When it comes to this service, there are two different strengths. They are 128 or 256 bit. 256 is going to be the best, so you will want to try to find a VPN with 256 bits. Additionally, you are going to want to find a VPN that allows you to choose your security settings. It is important to note that encryption tends to slow down network connections which means the strength of the encryption is going to help optimize connectivity in relation to security and speed. Of course, this all is dependent on what you plan to use the internet for as well.

You are also going to want to look for the size of the VPN network. It is important to locate a VPN with a minimum of fifty servers in the entire network. With more servers, available to use, you are going to have more access to bandwidth. Also, you will want to see what the system requirements and compatibility are. This is a simple step. All that needs to be done here is to ensure that the VPN is going to be compatible with every device you wish to connect it to. Most VPNs can be used with Mac or Windows operating systems. Ideally, you are going to want to find one that will also work with all your mobile devices, tablets included.

Finding a VPN that is easy to use is also crucial, especially when you are just starting to explore Tor and using the VPN as an added security measure. The easiest VPNs to use are those with automatic setups and those who have great customer service ratings just in case you need assistance. Below you are going to see a list of the top three rated VPNs among Dark Net users that are going to help you add protection to your internet searches.

HideMyAss – The name itself is quite funny, but we are going to talk about its attributes. This VPN comes with unlimited bandwidth, can be used on PC or Mac and with Linux or iOS. It is also able to be used on Android products. This service allows for two connections on each account, has 256-bit encryption, a worldwide network, live phone, chat, or email support available 24/7, and a thirty-day money back guarantee. The cons to this service are that it is known to be unreliable and sometimes slower than it should be. While it boasts 24/7 live support, their responses to email can be slow. Another con is that the software itself is a little more complicated than it should be, so beginners might want to shy away from this one.

Express VPN – This service gets a 9.5/10 rating among users. It offers the fastest connections and the strongest encryption available. Naturally, there are pros and cons with any service, and we will cover both, just as we did previously. Express VPN has more pros than cons, which is a great start. With this service, you will receive unlimited bandwidth, automatic setup, two connections with each account purchased, a worldwide network, compatibility with Android, iOS, Mac, Linux, and Windows. The connection is extremely reliable and very fast. It comes with the highest encryption at 256 bits and has options that are entirely customizable to your needs. They also offer 24/7 live chat support, a referral program, fast email responses and a money back guarantee. It seems that there is just one con with this service and it is that they do not offer any phone support. It is still highly rated and a favorite among users.

IPVanish – Overall, users of the VPN rate it 7/10, which is not a bad score. The connection is fast; you are allowed two connections per account, is compatible with Windows, Linux, Android, and Mac and has a worldwide network. The bandwidth matches the others with a 256-bit encryption. They offer a one week money back guarantee. IPVanish also provides a reliable, fast connection as well as an automatic setup. This VPN is not compatible with iOS, and while they say they have 24/7 email support, their responses tend to be slow. There is no phone support nor do they provide live chat options for assistance. In general, IPVanish does provide good connectivity, reliability, and speed. However, if you are using iOS, you are going to want to use either Express VPN or HideMyAss to get the coverage you need while using Tor.

There are many ways in which to conceal your online activities from those who have prying eyes. VPNs are one of the best ways to add an extra layer of protection to using the Tor network. Above are the highest rated VPNs.

Chapter 3

Using Tor for Online Anonymity

By now, you should have downloaded Tor, and this comment will address how to use Tor without VPNs or any other add-ons. Tor is easy to use. In this chapter, we will talk about how to use Tor and the differences you might see in the browser you just downloaded as opposed to what you are used to using. Tor is simple, but also incredibly different than what you are used to, and it is important you understand how to use it to avoid your information being compromised while surfing the web.

Once you have installed the browser on your computer or device, you will see a folder entitled *Tor Browser*. In there, you will find a link that is entitled *Start Tor Browser.exe*. Click on that link, and it will open a brand-new web browser. Next, you will be asked if you are sure you want to connect to the Tor network or if you would first prefer to configure your network settings. It is easiest if you choose to simply connect. There will be a few moments before the browser fully connects to the network. Once there, you will be able to surf the web anonymously.

If you want to be sure that you are correctly connected to the Tor network, you can connect to www.whatismyip.com. This is going to allow you to see where your IP address appears on a world map. If you are correctly connected to the Tor network, you should see your IP somewhere away from your home address. If you this, you are connected to Tor and ready to start securely browsing the internet.

Tor specifically is used to browse the internet safely and securely. However, it is important to keep in mind that you still have programs on your computer not protected by Tor. That means they are not secure and using them will make your information visible for anyone to see. Once you have the Tor browser installed, it is best to do everything through that browser. As we previously touched on, you will want to make sure you have a new virtual identity to avoid crossing the personal lines with those you wish to remain anonymous.

To explain how Tor works a little further, we are going to touch on site connections. The encryption process for this goes through the SSL or TSL. If encrypted sites are not being utilized, there is a risk of exposure to anyone who might be looking for this kind of mistake. There are always going to be people on Tor who are looking to exploit first time users. Before you get to looking through sites, make sure you have that anonymity. As we discussed in the VPN chapter, you can also add an extra browser powered by the Electronic Frontier Foundation that makes sure any sites used are going through the very secure SSL or TSL lines.

Always be careful of what kinds of sites you visit. Using Tor does not necessarily mean no one can see what you are doing, especially if you make one of the crucial mistakes we have previously discussed. Viruses and malware can still be installed on the computer if you do not pay attention to the kinds of sites you are accessing. Tor is meant to secure the sites you visit, not keep malicious attacks from happening. Making sure that your malware software is up to date is an important part of using Tor responsibly.

Most of us do not want others to know what we are researching online. It has nothing to do with the type of content we search and more to do with just wanting privacy, and there is nothing wrong with that. We all want to know that we are surfing the web anonymously. Without using Tor, anything you look at on the internet can be traced back to you. As we discussed previously, any ads related to sites you may have visited in the past are geared specifically toward you and are a result of the traffic analysis reports provided to marketing agencies. While we are doing nothing illegal, it is hard to imagine people being able to use information from websites we visit and create ads on our home screens or emails based on the sites we visited. Realistically speaking, we do not just have to worry about marketing either. Hackers, NSA, or FBI agents can easily see what we are doing online. As law-abiding citizens, we only need to worry about hackers who intend to do harm by stealing our personal information, which can be easily seen over the internet. Every day, hackers work hard to crack passwords for emails and bank accounts to take what we work so hard for.

The IP address you use in conjunction with your Wi-Fi is what tracks your online activity and is unique to you and the devices you use. The IP is associated with your computer and any devices used on that network. The provider is given your geographical location of whatever device is being used on the network. Every time you visit a website, the IP address pings on numerous servers which not only tells traffic analysis agents what kind of content you are searching but also where you are searching from.

In general, information sent over the servers lets the website know what kind of content to display. This includes the language it should be in, which is determined by where you are in the world. It also decides what kind of advertisements to show on the page, which is based on the types of websites you visit on a regular basis. Obviously, there will be websites you will want to refrain from visiting even while using Tor. Those include anything of a pornographic nature and those that government agencies might be watching. Anything related to treason or uprisings should always be avoided. There are also some keywords that when typed in a search engine (remember, we talked about avoiding using Google) that government agencies are specifically looking for. Even typing those into Tor could attract unwanted attention.

We touched earlier on the *geospoof*. This allows you to access services you may have been denied before based on your location. There are some countries that do not allow access to simple sites like MSN or Google, which is where Tor will come in handy. These along with VPNs can protect you from hackers while using public networks.

Chapter 4

How to use Tor Without Getting Caught

As we previously discussed, Tor is a volunteer operated network of people who provide people with secure and private ways to browse the web. Using Tor is done through a series of virtual tunnels and never makes a direct connection, which is what makes it hard for information on the Tor network to be traced. The use of indirect connections allows users to feel free to share any information they please through public networks and do not have to concern themselves with compromising their privacy. This also allows the user to access certain areas on the internet that are blocked otherwise.

Tor helps keep people safe from the most common ways others can see online activities, which is in the form of the aforementioned traffic analysis. Once Tor is downloaded (which at this point it should be) you will be able to avoid surveillance agencies and keep your internet activities concealed. Earlier, we talked about using Tor safely, and this chapter is going to go into a little more depth.

1. The most important rule is never to use Windows. Additionally, you will want to avoid using the Tor Browser bundle in conjunction with any Windows based program. The FBI exposed some of the vulnerabilities of Tor in their attempted takedown of Freedom Hosting. The Tor Browser Bundle has several vulnerabilities that are only exposed while using Windows based programs. Again, avoid Windows with Tor.

2. Download Linux. If you cannot create your workstation with Linux, there are other options available. Linux, in general, works best with Tor and can keep up with the updates Tor has on a regular basis. It also

works well with Privoxy and any firewalled web browsers on Clearnet. However, you can also try Whonix or Tails if Linux just is not compatible with your workstation. These applications take the guesswork and questions out of your searches and do all the work on your behalf. All outgoing access is firewalled, so third parties are unable to leak your data concerning what you are searching on the internet as well as your geographical location.

3. Make absolutely sure that all your storage is encrypted. LUKS is a great and very safe addition, and every Linux variation offers automated setup of this program during its installation process.

4. Always remember to keep your computer up to date. We touched on updating in a previous chapter, and it is incredibly important always to perform updates when prompted. If you are using Tails or you have

built a workstation on your own, you are going to want to update just to keep your vulnerabilities at the lowest risk levels. You can perform an update each time a new session is initiated, but at the very least you will want to update daily. Tails is great in that it will prompt you to update when the program starts if a vital update is necessary.

5. Disable Flash, JavaScript, and Java. Another one we touched on briefly before. If you come across a site that requires any of these, go to another site. There are plenty out there that do not require any of those programs to function properly. Those programs are used for traffic analysis, and you will want to avoid them, enabling them only as an absolute last resort. If you do enable any of those programs, make sure to disable it before leaving the site.

6. Always delete cookies and any local data being sent to you by a website. Tails nor Tor

can do this on their own and require some manual adjustments made by the user. You are also able to add on something known as *self-destructing cookies* which will take care of cookies on your behalf just in case you forget.

7. Never use Google as your primary search engine. This cannot be reiterated enough. You can use an engine known as *startpage* as that is the default search engine used on the Tor network, meaning it will be easy to access once you have the Tor browser. This search engine never requires the use of CAPTCHAs which is a great bonus.

8. Your workstation should always be a laptop. Being portable is important, and they are easy to destroy or dispose of in a pinch.

Another way to make sure your information is totally secure is to have a clean environment for your system to run. When we say clean, we do not mean dust free or clutter free. It is an environment in which you are not accessing regularly. These steps will ensure you are never at the same location, making it even harder to track your online searches.

1. Limit the amount of time you spend on Tor at any given location. Attacks of the correlation persuasion take a bit of time although they can be done in less than twenty-four hours. There are things known as Jackboots that rarely appear on the day you use Tor at a public location, but it is possible for them to be there the very next day. That is a great reason to avoid using Tor in the same place on a regular basis.

2. Avoid using Tor anywhere near your home. This is especially important if you are working on sensitive information. Even offline, computers tend to remain connected and often they can connect automatically. To truly keep prying eyes away from your system, do not use Tor longer than a full day

(24 hours) at any one location. Once you have used Tor at any given location, it is best to consider it trashed and move on. This works well even if Jackboots appear four to six months afterward. Again, it is always easier for people to remember the face of someone who comes in regularly over those they may have only seen once. If you do not have the convenience of living in a big city, consider traveling further out. It is difficult in smaller and sparsely populated towns, but it is doable if you want to protect your online identity.

3. Do not forget to leave your cell phone at home, turned on if you are going to be using Tor and do not want people to be able to track you.

This might sound weird, but it is good to have the correct mindset as it pertains to anonymity while using Tor and the Dark Net. Most users get caught for making an easy mistake like accidentally using their personal email address as opposed to the virtual reality email. You need to train yourself to have mental discipline when it comes to using Tor, and you will have nothing to worry about. Below are some ways you can work on training your mind.

1. If you plan on using any public Wi-Fi, you are going to have to make new accounts that match the pseudonym you created. If you have not created your virtual identity (pseudonym) yet, you are going to want to do that immediately. It is crucial to online safety and security. Never mix your online persona with your personal accounts. A good example is on Facebook. Make sure you never connect your real-life email address with the pseudonym for Instagram on the computer you use Tor. It will be much safer to wait until you get home.

2. On occasion, you will have to answer the phone. As we previously mentioned, it is

wise to have a prepaid phone. In some countries, it is a little more difficult than others, but always remember that where there is a will, there will be a way. Always pay in cash to both purchase the phone and purchase minutes. Never turn on the prepaid phone in a ten-mile radius of your home. Never use the phone if the battery cannot be removed. Do not insert a SIM card from any other device and never give out the number or admit to having a prepaid phone to anyone who is unaware of your pseudonym. It is hard to keep secrets from family members, but this does include them if they are unaware of your virtual identity.

3. Never do anything related to your pseudonym on Clearnet unless it is a last resort. For example, if you use a program that specifically prohibits the use of Tor (there aren't many, but they are out there). If you have to use this service, take added

steps to ensure your location is not visible to anyone.

Hidden services have been hotly debated and have made an appearance in the news lately. Recently, there was a takedown of two high-profile hidden services. Silk Road and Freedom Hosting were the sites involved. This turns out to be a bad/good news scenario. The bad news is that it shows the weaknesses in these hidden services. The good news is that the NSA does not seem all that interested in them.

Hidden services tend to be run under the control of another person meaning they can be compromised or vulnerable by another party. It is always important to make sure the anonymity of that service is protected because if it is compromised just one time, there is no going back.

The gist of this chapter is that it is difficult to have an online persona and a real-life persona. There is no technology in the world that can do this on its own. To be truly anonymous means you need to be able to take actions from the real world and mitigate weaknesses in the virtual world, pay attention to the little details and have a clear mind. There are some hackers who just happen upon information by sheer luck while others spend their entire day trying to bring down a network for no good reason. If a user makes a mistake that could have been avoided, it could have devastating consequences. While all of this may sound daunting, I implore you not to give up. Internet security is something we should all take an interest in and not simply because traffic analysis is performed and we are getting ads. There are malicious people out there looking to make another life hell. Keep working with Tor, and you will never look back.

Chapter 5

Using Bitcoins to Remain Anonymous

While remaining anonymous on the internet, you might have to use money to make purchases. It is incredibly difficult to manage funds or make purchases online while using a pseudonym. Thankfully, there is a remedy to that problem, and it is called Bitcoin. If used correctly, this service can keep your personal information safe and makes it next to impossible for anyone to be able to compare the online persona to that of the real-life person. Below, we are going to provide you with a step by step guide to setting up a Bitcoin account and how to use it. This will provide details on the Bitcoin environment, how you can communicate with others, browse the web anonymously and how to send or get Bitcoins.

1. The first step is to download Tails. It is on the Linux operating system that can be used

with a DVD or USB stick. You will not have to install this on a computer, which takes the anonymous level up a notch. Tails comes with all the software pre-installed on the disc or a USB drive. Once it is ready, it is going to route all traffic through the Tor network that you have already created. The best way to get Tails is from someone who already has a copy. They can transfer it onto a USB and hand it right over. You can also download it from their official Tails website. While it is not incredibly difficult, you will need to install it manually. Instructions are provided, and they are well written as well as easy to follow.

2. Fire Tails up. If you downloaded from the website, click on the link. Otherwise, you will insert the DVD or the USB to start Tails. Newer computers automatically detect the insertion of a new device and will ask to start up. There are occasions in which you will need to go through the BIOS startup. If

you have already set up your online persona (you certainly should have by now) you are going to want to use that when accessing Tails. Never use personal information. This includes browsing, chatting with other users, typing a document and Bitcoin transactions. Always keep your browsing focused and never log in to any personal media account while you are on Tails.

3. In this step, you are going to enable something called *persistence*. This step is required because without it you will be unable to save anything in Tails. There is a heading entitled Applications. From there you will select Tails and then choose the option to configure the persistent volume. For this option to work, the USB drive will be necessary to create the Tails Installer program. If you made the stick manually, it will be necessary to copy Tails with a different USB drive. The Tails installer process is found in Applications > Tails >

Tails Installer. From there, you will be required to create a passphrase. As with any passphrase, the longer it is the better because it will be more difficult to crack. Every time you use tails, you will be required to enter the passphrase so make sure it is something that is both lengthy and difficult for others, but easy for you to remember. During this process, Tails will ask you what information you want to store. Keep in mind that the less information stored within Tails, the more secure your connection will remain. Unfortunately, this also means you are going to have to remember which items you use in Tails and set them up each time you login to the service. The recommendation is that you use Bitcoin, Personal Data, GnuPG, Icedove, Network Connections, Pidgin, or Browser Bookmarks. Once you are done there, restart Tails with persistence enabled. Once again you must enter the passphrase. Anything done in the persistence folder can be saved when the computer is shut down.

4. Set up a KeePassX. This is a lifesaver for those of us using the Dark Net. It stores all your passwords meaning you will only be required to remember a couple. KeePassX is found under applications > accessories > KeePassX. You will need to create a password in this database by following the path: File > Create New Database. There is a program called Diceware that you can select a very long yet easily remembered password allowing access to KeePassX. This password will be the second of three passwords you will be required to remember. All passwords created from them on out will be remembered via KeePassX. This will be saved to the persistent folder. When creating a new password, you will click on the key (it should be yellow) and will say add new

47

entry. Give it a title and enter in the required information. The button you should pay attention to is called Gen, which is on the right side of the Repeat field. Select Gen by clicking the button and it will generate a password on your behalf. You can determine the length of the password and if you want it to have special numbers or characters. To keep things at the highest level of secure, it is best if you do not even look at the password. There is no need to see it or know it since it will be saved for you. If by some chance someone is looking at your screen, all that can be seen is stars and not the password itself. Generating the password is automated. Once it is done, copy and paste it into the site you need to access.

5. The next step is to get a PGP Key. In Tails, you will have to make a new PGP Key which can be found by clicking Applications then Utilities followed by Passwords and Keys.

Next, you are going to click the symbol that looks like a blue plus sign. That can be found under the GnuPG key. From there, enter your name and email address. Make sure it is the pseudonym you created, especially if you intend on sending encrypted emails. The password here will be required each time you need to decrypt a file, or an encrypted email is sent to you.

6. From there you will set up Electrum. In your Bitcoin Wallet, you can click on applications > Internet > Bitcoin Wallet. Electrum is thought of as a lightweight wallet according to Bitcoin standards. You will not need a copy of Blockchain, and it relies instead on other types of nodes. Several nodes, in fact. If you wish to see your balance, you can enter the bitcoin address into your Blockexporlorer. This is done by using Blockcypher so you can see your balance and any transactions that occurred with the Bitcoin account. It is in this area you will

create your wallet. There is no need for anything other than the standard wallet, which works perfectly fine. In there you will see thirteen words typed in English that are representative of the wallet seed. Anyone with that seed combination can access your wallet and steal Bitcoins from it. It is important you are very careful with where you store those thirteen words. With KeePassX already installed, it will be easy to store the words in that program securely. You can also write them down and lock the combination of words away if you find it difficult to paste it in the comment field. Press the proceed button and you will be able to put the wallet seed in the window that pops up. After that, choose your password. Again, we recommend you create one with KeePassX. This password will be required for every transaction. With that setup, you will be able to send and get Bitcoin payments. Addresses and balances as they relate to the Bitcoin can be found under the addresses heading. What is great here is you can also create more than one wallet under the same identity. You are also able to create a new wallet just for a single transaction. Keeping your wallets separate makes it much simpler to keep money separated for accounting purposes or for your privacy in general.

7. Next you will want to use the XMPP and OTR to communicate. Pidgin is the program used when chatting with other users. It is difficult to get an anonymous email account, so some find it easier to chat with people by using the Pidgin tool. There is one issue with this in that you cannot get messages when you are not online. You can install Pidgin by going to Applications > Internet > Pidgin. After that, you are going to be able to access Pidgin, add your account and then check XMPP as your protocol. Many of the XMPP servers are public. To provide an accurate

example, we selected the search engine entitled duckduckgo for its privacy friendly standards. Once there, you can choose your user name and enter duckgo.com for the domain. Next, you will choose a password and select the box entitled *create new account on the server*. Close the window and reconnect so the new chat account with Pidgin is enabled. When the window is reopened, it might ask you to reenter your user name and password. Once again, we will mention KeePassX for this. It is much easier to store them there rather than having so many to remember. To use the secure chat function, select the OTR encryption option. You will do that by clicking OTR > Start Private Conversation. You can also choose to verify the integrity by clicking OTR > Authenticate Buddy.

8. In this step, you are going to make sure that you back everything up by using PGP. Of all the steps, this is the trickiest because it

takes some effort. The more of your effort put into locking the key means that it will be less accessible should you need it. We recommend a very strong password by using Diceware when you create the PGP Key. The key can be loaded onto any USB device and left with friends or a family member, or a lawyer or safe deposit box if necessary. We also recommend that a regular backup of all documents you do not want to lose is done. This also applies to KeePassX and your Bitcoin wallet. Select all files and the folders you want to backup. From there, right-click the selection and click encrypt. You may see a popup window asking which keys you would like to encrypt. From there, you will only need to select the PGP key. It is important to avoid clicking the sign option. When it comes time to decrypt a file, all you will need to do is double click the file labeled .gpg then enter the password for the PGP key.

9. The last step in this process is to repeat all steps one through eight for each identity created. There will need to be different USB drives with Tails for every pseudonym you create. Each stick should have a different password, separate KeePassX databases, and different PGP keys.

Now that we have those steps completed, we can briefly touch on how to get Bitcoins. In this case, you should remember and be aware that no matter how you acquire the Bitcoins, the actual transaction is difficult to keep entirely anonymous. For your convenience, we have detailed a few of those options below that show a more private way to make Bitcoin transactions.

Bitcoins can be purchased in person through what are known as bitcoin meetups which are found under the marketplace option under the Mycelium wallet. This is only something that can be done on the Android version. You are also able to find traders with local Bitcoin platforms.

You can also get Bitcoins from an ATM. There are many of these in countries all over the world, and alternatively, there are countries in which Bitcoin ATMs are incredibly rare. You can find the Coin ATM Radal to locate Bitcoin ATMs in your area. You will need to click on the *other services* option on the left-hand corner, or you could miss places that offer to sell Bitcoins as vouchers.

If you choose to spend bitcoins, you should also accept them as a form of payment. In doing this, acquiring them will be an unnecessary step. Bitcoins received are not anonymous because somewhere there is a record that they were paid to you. It is a bit of a double-edged sword. If you are looking for convenience and it does not matter if there is a record, accept bitcoins as a form of payment. If anonymity is more important, finding Bitcoin ATMs is the way to go.

The last thing we will talk about in this chapter is mining bitcoins. This is not the most profitable way to get them but is a fine alternative. To mine

Bitcoins, you will need a mining machine paid for with cash. You will have to plug it in, point it toward the mining pool, and watch the earnings come to you.

Chapter 6

Web Levels and Pseudonyms

Because we have mentioned it a couple of times, and because it is important, we are going to touch briefly on the use of Dark Net personas. The Dark net is the internet that is hidden beneath the actual internet and purposely kept from the view of people who are considered *ordinary* web users. One of the most normal misconceptions is that the Dark Net is hard to access, which as you should know by now is untrue. Using the Dark Net requires no special skill or knowledge, you simply have to download the TOR browser, and you are good to go.

Before we get into pseudonyms, we will cover what the differences are between deep web, dark web, and the surface web. The surface web is the easiest. That is the internet most people are used to using. One can find anything they need by using search engines like Safari and Bing. The deep web is a level more complicated. People are not always able to find things that are easily accessible on the surface web with the standard search engines. These tend to be things like government databases and online libraries. Then, we have the dark web. It is like the dark corner of a room, intentionally kept hidden with the use of normal search engines. This is where the Tor network is, which is why you can only access the dark web by using the Tor browser.

Being anonymous on the dark net is done by using the onion network. The standard internet directly accesses servers that are set up to host whatever website the user is visiting. When using an onion network, direct links are broken intentionally, and the data is sent through several pipelines or intermediaries before it gets to the final destination. The result is the same because you will ultimately reach the website you originally searched for. The medium through which the routes are transported is what prevents others from seeing who or what is behind the communication that was sent. Tor uses the onion router, and it is meant to be an anonymous and user friendly way to communicate with any operating system.

Originally, the dark net was invented by the US military. Law enforcement organizations, the government, and people in the military are some of the most common users of the dark net. They use browsers like Tor because the surface web makes it easy for others to see the near exact location of the user, even when the best encryption techniques are put in place. This is what helps protect agents who are out working in the field as well as politicians or soldiers in need of keeping their negotiations from being seen by others.

The dark net is also particularly popular with bloggers and journalists, generally those who are living in countries where censorship and the possibility of being imprisoned for political speech against said country are prohibited. Remaining anonymous online helps to keep all those people safe and allows them to communicate with other people as well as have access to information that may be blocked by firewalls. The dark net is also a platform for revolutionaries or activists who want to organize marches or protests without fear of retaliation from the government they oppose or revealing their location to anyone who may be watching.

Tor, which also stands for The Onion Router, is quite easy to access. It is also the most common platform used to access the dark net. If you are the kind of person who is technologically inclined, you can configure Tor to meet your specific needs. And if tech savvy is not something you are good at, that is okay too. Tor is easy for anyone to access and use. Tor is built on top of the Firefox internet browser, which most of us are familiar with already.

Tor gives its users added protection against government agencies who may be spying to collect information, traffic analysis and it also protects against hackers. Tor lets the user access sites that were purposely published with anonymity. Those are the most popular and frequently searched websites on the dark net.

A little earlier we briefly mentioned the Freenet Project, which is a browser similar to Tor. Through Freenet, one can create a private network in which any resource located or provided on the computer will only be accessible by those who have been placed on a list of friends. The I2P (Invisible Internet Project) is also similar in that it provides file sharing plugins, secure email servers, file storage and features geared toward social activities like blogging or chat.

Now, when you are ready to create your online persona, this is the place to let your imagination run wild. What is great about pseudonyms is you can call yourself whatever you like. If it is your intention to appear legitimate or conduct business using the dark net, you can also use a name that would be considered more common. Either way, you are free to do as you please. If you find yourself stuck, there are sites that can generate some interesting names on your behalf. and you can almost guarantee it will give you a name that has not yet been used on the dark net. Whatever name you choose can be used for the email address, Bitcoins, or screen names on Tor.

Chapter 7

Tor Weaknesses

This is not what we want to think of when accessing a web that is supposed to be secure, but everything has a weakness, and we are going to cover the weaknesses of Tor so you can avoid them and feel safe using the dark net.

Like anything else in life, Tor has boundaries. It can provide protection against traffic analysis but cannot prevent the traffic from being confirmed. Some of the most common weaknesses are that of eavesdropping and below we are going to talk about the different kinds of eavesdropping.

The autonomous system, also known as AS, are segments used for exit or entry and relaying information for the destination site. Autonomous systems make it so traffic on those segments will interfere with communications between the end destination and the user.

Next, there is Exit Node Eavesdropping. Without being careful, the usernames, passwords, and Bitcoin information of the user can be intercepted if the person on the other end simply watches the exit nodes, which is where the data exits. Tor is unable to encrypt everything going out the exit node because the end to end encryption was never put in place. This type of eavesdropping does not breach the anonymity of Tor, but it does make it easier for people who may be watching to catch information on the exit nodes and use that information to decipher a location of the user. It can also be used for less nefarious reasons like traffic analysis, which simply aims to advertise to the user's likes and avoid their dislikes.

Another kind of attack is one we have mentioned a few times, and that is the traffic analysis. Advertisers get a peek at the traffic on the Tor network by looking at those exit nodes. They decide which ones to keep an eye on and use the information to advertise accordingly. It is not a malicious attack and is only meant to prompt the user to spend a little money online through their website. The traffic analysis also reveals the location of the user, and it can provide basic information like name and email or even phone numbers.

There is also the exit node push. This is where a person operating a site can choose to refuse data to enter the nodes. They can also reduce the number of users allowed on the network. An example of this is being unable to edit websites like Wikipedia through the Tor network.

Next, we have what is known as the bad apple attack. This is done through using BitTorrent while using the Tor network. A user's IP address can be revealed through BitTorrent by taking advantage of Tor. The severity of the attack depends on the exit node control. On occasion, there could be a secondary attack so the user and their IP address or location can be fully exploited.

Another common attack is the exposure of the IP address. Through this method, there is a dissimulation technique that allows people to control the exit node. This was part of a research study that showed in twenty-three days there were three attacks that successfully exploited the system and revealed IP addresses.

Unfortunately, there are ways that Tor can be hacked, but the risk is minimal so long as you follow proper protocols.

Chapter 8

Staying Concealed While Using the Internet

There are quite a few ways to conceal yourself while surfing the web, a few of which we have discussed previously. There are some that are obvious such as the use of an incognito or private browser. There is another option that is less frequently discussed, and that is to kill cookies. This action does not kill supercookies, which we will discuss a little later, but it can keep your browsing anonymous while browsing the standard internet. One of the best ways to rid your computer of cookies is to use Ccleaner, a free downloadable program from the internet. It can delete flash and cookies.

You can also search anonymously by turning off the personalized search on whichever search engine you use. Whether it is Google or Bing, there is the option to turn off the search. You may have noticed when typing in the first few letters; most search engines will try to complete the sentence for you. That is the personalized search option. To turn this off, you will go to Search Tools then click on All Results and then Verbatim. This provides some anonymity, but not as much as it would if you used just the dark net. You can also choose to use search engines that are private, one of which we discussed earlier called duckduckgo.

You can also stop Google from tracking your location and keeping track of your searches. If you were not aware that this was happening, consider yourself informed. Google has so many options like calendars, Gmail, and Google plus that it can build profiles based on the services you use through its servers. Google uses a unified privacy policy which simply means that it can legally track you across any service. Unfortunately, that means they can scan emails, and it will use that data to personalize the ads from advertisers. Your profile photo can also appear on items you may have liked while you were logged into your Gmail account or Google Plus. This is something you can opt out of and is done by simply turning off all personalized ads. You are also allowed to download the Google Analytic Browser Add-on which will cease the collection of data based on the places you searched on the internet, which Google will later sell to their ad partners.

You are also able to block trackers on the internet. Each site on the web has cookies that are made just to track activity embedded in the site. Sponsored links, comment boxes, and ads are all examples of cookies that are embedded and used for tracking purposes. You can use anti-tracking plugins such as Privacy Badger, Ghostery, and Disconnect that are used specifically to block cookies made to track. This keeps analytic companies from building profiles based on the kinds of sites you visit while surfing the web. Any of those programs listed above are easily found and downloadable from the internet. Once they are put in place, they do the work for you and destroy tracking cookies before they even know what hit them.

There is also the option of a proxy network. Many of the options we have discussed in this chapter are great for dodging cookies but frequented websites, and online activity is still tracked by your browser's IP address. These IP addresses can help give an approximate location of the computer or tablet, and it lets the trackers know how often you go to specific websites. To get some more privacy, you can consider downloading the VPNs we talked about previously. There is another option known as CyberGhost, which is cheap and is compatible with PC, Mac, iOS, and Android.

Of course, there is the option to download an anonymous browser and is something that should be seriously considered. Plugins and proxies, as well as trying to recall whether you are using a private browsing session, can lead to a frustrating and extended web browsing environment. A lot of us get accustomed to using a certain kind of browser, and if that is something you can let go of, you can download a new browser as another option. Doing this allows the user to turn on their proxy networks with switches that are found in the toolbar. One of these is the Epic browser, which was modeled after Chrome. The privacy settings are incredibly high, and third party cookies are always blocked. Users can search whatever sites they like, and browsing is never tracked. You are going to see ads still, but the activity and sites you visit will not be logged. There is a neat counter on the homepage that will let you know how many times a tracker tried to log your activities in one day. It is a cool feeling to see that every attempt to track your activity was thwarted by the browser you use.

You can also consider services that provide data removal. There is a product called *DeleteMe* which costs around one-hundred dollars per year. That fee includes the deletion of all information collected by companies that will, in turn, sell it to other advertisers. The only pitfall to this is you must pay for it. Also, it does not necessarily remove every bit of information from the searches, which leaves the user slightly vulnerable.

While it is not common knowledge, you can hide your IP address by using an IP scrambler. One of the most common programs is called Virtual World Computing Cocoon. This will show the user as a *cocoon user* to those who may be spying. It is considered a smart proxy, and when logging into Cocoon, the IP address on the site is the only thing that is seen, not the actual IP address of the person using Cocoon. This is a great service capable of protecting those who use Wi-Fi networks in public places.

You also have the option to disallow social networks to track your internet activity. Any time you click like on something on Facebook or Twitter, information on that is stored in massive databases and used to form ads based on your likes. If you would like to remove that from Facebook, you simply go to the privacy settings and click on adverts to control. By removing that option, the things you like on Facebook can no longer be tracked. Any social media site has this option, and unless you are unable to live without social media entirely, we strongly suggest you remove those options from all your social media outlets.

Because most of us are unable to completely stop using the internet or social media in general, this chapter has been geared toward finding other alternatives to browsing anonymously. This is for those using unsecured computers or tablets that have not got the option to download Tor. You will want to be able to use Tor to avoid being spied on while surfing the internet.

Chapter 9

Encryption and Supercookies

We briefly mentioned supercookies in the previous chapter, and this one is going to go over them in a little more detail. First, let us define what a regular cookie is. Unfortunately, we are not discussing the chocolate chip persuasion. HTTP cookies are known as a regular or simple cookie. It is code downloaded to a user's internet browser each time they reach a website. Those cookies can store information useful to the user, and the website can track interactions between the user and the website they reached. A good way to describe how this works is using Amazon to shop. Any item left in your cart are stored using a cookie so if you leave the website without making the purchase, those things stay in the cart for when you return. The cookie will send information to Amazon when you return to the site later.

Cookies are also able to let a website know the user is logged in, so the user does not have to input their login information repeatedly. The third-party cookies can track users across the internet and gather information to sell to marketing companies by simply letting them know what types of websites the user visited while online.

Now, a super cookie is like a tracking cookie, but it is much more complicated.

If you want to keep cookies from tracking your activity online, clearing the browsing history is a simple way to keep this from happening. It is a simple step and can clear every cookie that was previously stored on the computer. The only issue that creates is the user must input all their login information each time they visit, and any items left in virtual shopping carts will no longer be stored. That is good in that the cookies will not be able to track your activity but bad in that it causes extra steps each time you log in.

That technique will not work with the supercookies. They are not a standard cookie stored within the browser. There is information unique to the connection of the specified user that will be entered in the header of the HTTP by the internet service provider. That information can identify whatever website the user visited. Information between the server and the device being used means the user is unable to do anything about it. This information will not be stored on any device and hence cannot be deleted. Any ad blocking software mentioned is unable to block a supercookie.

Supercookies are particularly dangerous because of the violation of privacy that may occur. In general, cookies on any single website are not shared with another website. UIDH can be revealed to all websites, and that is where tons of information regarding internet searches, history and habits are stored. The supercookie is something that advertisers can use to find all deleted cookies from the device and then link them to new cookies.

The supercookie sounds like a mosquito that just cannot be killed. They can keep tons of information about your personal life and revive all the cookies you deleted that should not be stored on any of your personal devices. There is not much that can be done about the supercookie except to use VPNs. We talked about the top three previously, and in addition to using the Tor network, VPNs are a great added layer of security to keep those pesky cookies and supercookies from tracking and storing your activity and information.

VPNs work well on computers, but not handheld devices like smartphones or tablets, which tend to be at higher risk for supercookies. If you are using your phone to browse the internet, there is the option to use proxy settings that are encrypted. ISPs can remove that encryption, so you need to be careful to make sure they are in place each time you use your phone to browse the web.

It is an unfortunate fact that the options are limited when it comes to using your smartphone or tablet to search the web. Using an untraceable phone or avoiding using the internet while on your phone are going to be your best bets, even if they are difficult to imagine.

Chapter 10

Tor and Hacking

Hacking, in general, is considered illegal and yet is something done regularly through Tor as well as any other browser. Tor can be used to hack any application, but it is more difficult and requires slightly more patience. Hacking, in general, requires diligence and stealth as well.

Once you have downloaded the Tor browser (which undoubtedly you have by now), configure it in a manner that works best for you. Commonly Tor users simply allow Tor to set all the configurations through the setup process. If there is anything specific you wish to do during this process, there is undoubtedly a way to do so. Remember, anything done through the setup can be changed later to meet your needs.

As previously discussed, it is wise to test the network and ensure you are using Tor and not the standard web. To access the deep web, you will find deepweb.pw on the Tor URL bar. From there, you are going to be able to access services such as TorSearch, Hidden Wiki, and Tails.

Once you are in the deep Web, you can use those tunnels through Tor and access other websites that cannot be discovered on the standard web. Users are also able to add on tools to their browser that are going to be added layers of protection when it comes to activities on the dark net. The add-ons users are going to want to look for are Page Hacker and HackBar. Both of those are going to allow access to even deeper parts of the dark net.

Below are some steps for hacking into any system. The difference here is that it is being done through Tor and those add-ons we mentioned previously. Please note that hacking is an illegal activity. The purpose of this section is to simply be informative and should only be used for educational purposes.

1. Find the *nix terminal to use on all commands. Cygwin is one of the better

programs and can mimic nix for users on a Windows system. (Remember that previously we stated Windows and Tor are not the best of friends. However, this is an alternative if Windows OS is your only option).

2. Ensure the computer that is going to be hacked is secure. Before starting, it is important to make sure your system is entirely secure, so a counter hack does not occur. Also, there needs to be little to no possibility that the person being hacked can trace the hack back to the user. Part of the reason behind this tutorial section is to enable the user to see if their own system is hackable. That is the most legal way to check the security of your own system, and it is a neat technique to learn in the process.

3. Ensure the user has the ping utility tool so a target activity can be tested. There is a flaw in this tool in that the administrator of the

system might be alerted and can shut the system down before any hacking takes place.

4. Scan the ports on the target system. There should be a list of all open ports provided from the ping tool in step three. In this step, the user is also going to be able to determine the kind of firewall in place in addition to the type of router used on the target system.

5. Ports like the FTP or HTTP are less protected and easily accessible or exploited. Open ports for LAN gaming are DUP or TCP and are also easier to access. From here the user is going to see SSH, which is secure shell service, running on the target system. On occasion, the user can force those ports open using brute force, which will allow access to them as well.

6. Finding the password. This is one of the more difficult steps, but this is also where brute force attack comes in. This will crack

the password and allow access to the system.

These are the first steps used to hack into another system while in the Tor network. As hacking is illegal, these steps are general and meant to provide guidance to the user so they can ensure their systems are safe. It is not intended to hack into another system.

In this chapter, we are also going to provide some information on staying safe while using Tor as it seems fitting. Below are some precautions everyone should take to stay safe while using the dark net. Always keep in mind that while you are searching the net using Tor, there are authorities and hackers who are doing the same and they are attempting to discover who is hosting certain websites and what people may be accessing criminal sites as well. The basics are listed below.

1. First and foremost, use that pseudonym. You are going to want to remain as anonymous as possible. This cannot be

stressed enough. Tor is used for anonymity so using your real information or profiles defeats the purpose of going to it all together.

2. Tor is slightly slow because of the sheer number of nodes that it must pass through. It is wise to use a VPN to give yourself that added layer of security when browsing the dark net.

3. Always disable scripts that are running. This is an option in Tor as well as any standard web browser. Most sites on the dark net are considered criminal, and if you accidentally find yourself visiting one, the online authorities may want to try to track you down. Scripts were created with JavaScript, and as we previously discussed, Java or JavaScript should not be enabled while using the standard web let alone Tor. Those are meant to store things on your

computer, which is exactly what using Tor is meant to avoid.

4. Always think twice before clicking links because they may not be what they appear or claim to be. Some of the search engines can appear misleading. Tor has its own search engines including duckduckgo, which we previously mentioned as well as Torch. If you are looking to research information and want to do so without worry, Tor has a library that is great for this purpose. That way you know you will avoid clicking into something you never intended. Inside the Tor library, you will also find tons of hidden search engines meant to add to the security and safety of using the Tor network. If this is your first time accessing Tor, the library is the best place to start.

5. Never download anything directly to your computer. This includes BitTorrents because they can provide the actual IP

address for the user as it is meant to store things on a computer. That will make your activity traceable to you and can mean trouble if you are not careful.

Chapter 11

Using Tor to Avoid Marketers or Debt Collectors

At some point in our lives, many us have had the unfortunate pleasure of being indebted to collectors. Those debt collectors are particularly meddlesome and often call your place of employment or relatives just to try to track you down. Hiding from debt collectors is not going to dissolve the debt, and it is not an end all be all solution. It is simply a way to get relief from the harassing phone calls and incessant emails, so you have a moment to breathe and find a way to get yourself out of debt.

If it is difficult for debt collectors and marketers to find you, they will not be able to continue their harassment. One way to do this is to change your address. It is difficult to up and move, not to mention expensive. A way around this is to set up a PO Box. Always keep in mind that you are responsible for the debt that has been amassed. Once the PO Box in place, you can call all the creditors and change your address. They will try to ask for a physical address, but you are not legally required to give it to them.

Next, get yourself one of those disposable phones. They are cheap and have prepaid minutes. There is no contract requirement, and they can be bought anywhere from gas stations to Walmart. Because they are so cheap, you can have one for family and friends and another for those bill collectors. When you find yourself tired of all the phone calls, shut the designated bill collector phone off and take a moment to breathe.

Where does Tor come in, you ask? Right now. Earlier we talked about cookies and supercookies and all the activity that are traced on the standard web. Limiting your footprint online is a great way to hide from those collectors. You might be surprised to know that marketers and bill collectors look to social media accounts to find people. Refrain from posting personal information. Set all social media profiles like Facebook, Twitter, or Instagram to private. When doing this on Facebook specifically, anyone who is not a friend cannot contact you. Remember that pictures can speak a thousand words and provide clues as to where you may be. Photos taken on smartphones can also have the coordinates embedded in them, which might provide marketers or collectors with your geographical location.

If you apply for credit online, you will be required to give information like your physical address, social security number, and income. You can avoid risking this information being leaked by using Tor. The dark net is specifically intended to keep your personal information personal, and it is a great tool to use if you find yourself in need of applying for a line of credit. Unless you can avoid applying for credit in general, it is best to use Tor, so all information provided is kept private and not used for marketing.

Again, we previously discussed the importance of using the dark net to conceal activities and keep marketers from targeting you personally. To add that extra layer of protection, we implore you to consider the VPNs discussed in a previous chapter. The ideas discussed here will help to alleviate some of the stress but remember they are not fool proof.

Chapter 12

Using Tor to Avoid the NSA or Spies

One of the main government agencies dedicated to watching internet traffic is the NSA. They have people who keep an eye out for specific words or phrases that are meant to catch terrorists. While the clear majority of us are not using the internet for nefarious reasons, some of those words or phrases might be used without meaning harm at which point you may have caught the attention of agents of the NSA. Just like we do not want marketers or bill collectors to track us online, we certainly do not want to get the attention of the NSA. Using Tor is a great way to browse the internet without fear of accidentally saying something or using a catch word unintentionally.

Throughout this book, we have talked about added layers of security. Tor is not infallible, nor is there any other system out there that is. In addition to VPNs, users can use AsToria, which is a tool specifically for Tor which keeps prying eyes from seeing the type of information you are trying to access on the web.

AsToria was developed to allow Tor users a way to rid themselves of systems that will try to hack into the Tor network and reveal identities of those using the web anonymously. AsToria specifically works to fight against timed attacks against Tor. Algorithms were built into AsToria to protect against the worst-case scenario situations of cyber attack. AsToria consistently checks for and sends the user on the best and clearest route so they cannot be traced.

AsToria is an add on for Tor, just like the VPNs we discussed. In all honesty, while many government agencies use Tor, they would like to see it taken down for the common folk so they can easily see what everyone is doing online. They have tried several times to breach Tor and bring the network down and have not been successful.

However, that is another reason to get those added security layers. It is one more wall any government agency would have to leap over to get to your IP address or geographical location. Any perceived weakness will be exploited, and Tor is designed to keep weaknesses at a minimum so its users can freely search whatever they please, post whatever political blogs they like and gather their fellow activists without fear of retaliation.

When used properly, Tor is perfectly capable of concealing your online activity. We briefly covered hacking in the Tor network, so users were aware it was a possibility. There will always be agencies or people looking to exploit others or simply see what they are searching for online.

For the most part, the NSA does not concern themselves with law-abiding citizens. So long as you are not continuously searching things on their watch list, there is nothing to worry about. We have all mistyped something and feared the worst, but no NSA agent ever came knocking on our door.

They do have serious matters to attend to, which sometimes includes attempts at bringing down the Tor network.

Overall it is important to remember Tor is a wonderfully secret place you can go to search the dark net for things you might not be able to find anywhere else. It is intended to allow those types of searches as well as providing online anonymity to anyone who wishes to use it. Tor, in addition to the added layers of security, will make it easy for people to research or perform business transactions online without having to worry about their personal information being tracked and sold to the highest bidder. It is a wonderful invention for people simply wishing to exercise their right to browse freely.

Other Books by Author

Bitcoin: How to Get, Send and Receive Bitcoins Anonymously

Python Programming: A Step by Step Beginner's guide to Coding with Python in 7 Days or Less!

Hacking with Python: Your Guide to Ethical Hacking, Basic Security, and Python Hacking

Wireless Hacking: How to Hack Wireless Networks

You can find Evan Lane's books at:
http://bit.ly/evanlane